# Why are pandas in peril?

## Barbara Taylor

First published in 2011 by Miles Kelly Publishing Ltd
Harding's Barn, Bardfield End Green, Thaxted,
Essex, CM6 3PX, UK

2 4 6 8 10 9 7 5 3 1

**Publishing Director** Belinda Gallagher
**Creative Director** Jo Cowan
**Editorial Director** Rosie McGuire
**Editor** Sarah Parkin
**Volume Designer** Liz Wiffen (Punch Bowl Design)
**Cover Designer** Kayleigh Allen
**Image Manager** Liberty Newton
**Indexer** Gill Lee
**Production Manager** Elizabeth Collins
**Reprographics** Anthony Cambray, Stephan Davis

ISBN 978-1-84810-458-7

Printed in China

British Library Cataloguing-in-Publication Data

A catalogue record for this book is
available from the British Library

**ACKNOWLEDGEMENTS**
The publishers would like to thank the following
artists who have contributed to this book:

Mike Foster (character cartoons), Ian Jackson (dodo)

All other artwork from the Miles Kelly Artwork Bank

The publishers would like to thank the following
sources for the use of their photographs:

**FLPA** 29 Ariadne Van Zandbergen
**iStockphoto.com** 8 Jan Will; 28 Christine Eichin
**Shutterstock.com** 13 Sam Chadwick;
14 Oleksii Abramov; 19 worldswildlifewonders;
22 Karen Givens; 24–25 Eric Gevaert

All other photographs are from:
digitalvision, PhotoDisc

Every effort has been made to acknowledge the
source and copyright holder of each picture.
Miles Kelly Publishing apologises for any unintentional
errors or omissions.

Made with paper from a sustainable forest

www.mileskelly.net
info@mileskelly.net

www.factsforprojects.com

# contents

# what are endangered animals?

**They are very rare animals that will die out soon without our help.** If an animal, such as a tiger, is endangered it means there are very few of them left in the world and they are in danger of being wiped out completely.

Tigers

# Do eagles need our help?

Yes they do. Eagles are having trouble surviving because we have built farms, mines and cities in their natural homes. Humans have also hunted and poisoned these rare birds, and collected their eggs.

Philippine eagle

## Poo reveals all!

Endangered animals' poo reveals a lot about what they eat and how healthy they are. This information can help scientists to stop rare animals from dying out.

# How many animals die out every day?

Up to 300 animal types probably die out every day – especially small ones such as bugs. About half of all the world's insects are in danger of dying out right now.

## Draw

Can you think of five different bugs? Using books to help you, draw pictures of your five bugs.

# Will I ever see a dinosaur?

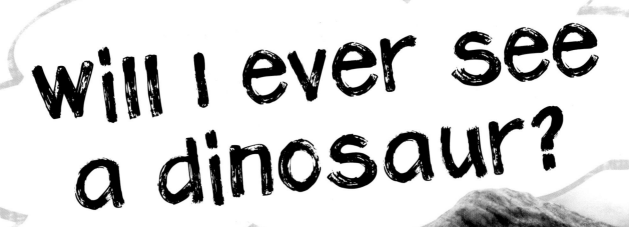

**Nobody will ever see a real living dinosaur.** They died out millions of years before people lived on Earth. Dinosaurs ruled the world for over 150 million years and developed into over 1000 different types.

*Tyrannosaurus rex*

# why did the dinosaurs die out?

It may have been because a huge space rock hit Earth. Dust thrown into the air would have blocked out the sunlight. The dinosaurs could not have survived because the animals that they ate would have also died out.

## Going, going, gone!
More than 99 out of every 100 animals that ever lived are extinct and will never walk the Earth again.

# Can we save the dodo?

No we can't — they are gone forever. Dodos were large birds that lived on an island in the Indian Ocean. The last one was killed over 300 years ago. When the last of a particular kind of animal dies out and has not been seen in the wild for 50 years, it is classed as extinct.

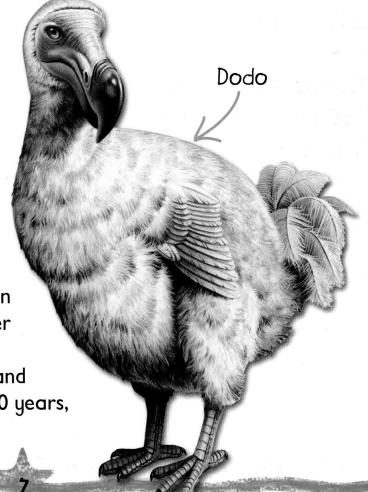

Dodo

# why do polar bears need ice?

**Polar bears hunt on the ice that covers the Arctic Ocean, so they need it to live.** The bears wait for seals to come up for air at holes in the ice. Now the world is warming up and the ice is melting, polar bears find it more difficult to catch food and are becoming rare.

Polar bear

### Bird thief!

Many birds are rare in the wild because their eggs or chicks are stolen from their nests. The chicks are often sold as pets.

# which porpoise might disappear?

The vaquita, the smallest type of porpoise, is in danger of disappearing. There are less than 250 of these shy animals left. Vaquitas are often drowned in fishing nets or killed by boats. Pollution is also a danger to them.

Vaquita

## Paint

The polar bear's favourite food is seals. Paint a picture of your favourite food.

# why do people destroy animal homes?

There are seven billion people on our planet that all need somewhere to live and food to eat. People chop down forests, plough up grasslands and drain swamps to build houses and farms, but these places are also animal homes. If animals don't have anywhere to live, they will die out.

# where do lemurs live?

Lemurs live on an island called Madagascar, which is cut off from the rest of the world. They are found nowhere else in the wild and are becoming rare. If people don't protect them, they will become extinct.

Ring-tailed lemur

## Draw

Imagine you are an explorer visiting an island. Draw a rare animal that lives there.

# which snail was wiped out?

The partula snail was wiped out after people took a killer snail to some islands in the South Pacific Ocean. They wanted it to eat the giant African snails that were destroying crops but it ate partula snails instead.

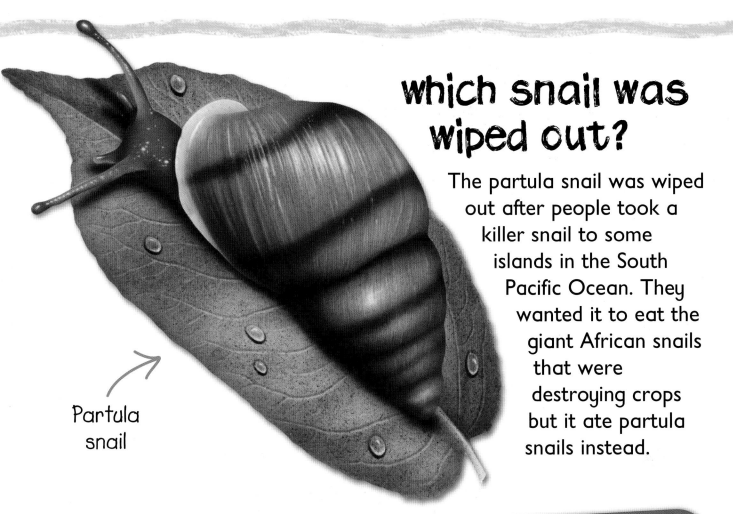

Partula snail

## celebrity for two days!

People thought that solenodons had died out on the island of Cuba, but one was suddenly found! It was studied for two days and released back into the wild.

# Do tigers have pouches?

No they don't! However there was a pouched animal called the Tasmanian tiger, or thylacine. They were called tigers because of their striped coats. Due to hunting, disease and the loss of its home, it is now extinct.

# Why did people hunt whales?

**Whales were once hunted for their bones and fatty blubber.** Even the fringed plates in their mouths were used to make umbrellas and tennis rackets. The northern right whale has never recovered from being hunted.

Northern right whale →

## Discover

Find out how much a blue whale weighs when it is born. How much did you weigh as a baby?

# Do seals wear fur coats?

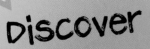

Northern fur seals have thick, soft fur, which was once used to make fur coats. Sadly, many were killed and their numbers dropped.

## Tangled underwater!

Dolphins may get tangled up in fishing nets. If they become trapped underwater, they will drown.

# Which whales are rare?

Despite being protected from hunters, seven out of the 13 great whales are still endangered. These are the humpback whale, blue whale, bowhead whale, fin whale, northern right whale, sei whale and sperm whale.

Humpback whale

# Which dragon is in danger?

**The leafy sea dragon.** This strange animal isn't actually a dragon — it is a fish! Its leaf-like body makes it look like seaweed and helps it to hide from its enemies. They are rare because people collect them to keep as pets or make medicines.

Leafy sea dragon

## Hide

Dress as a leafy sea dragon and try to blend into the background. Can anyone find you?

## strange soup!

Millions of sharks are killed just for their fins, which are used to make shark fin soup. Sharks are the rarest group of animals in the oceans.

## can fish live in caves?

A fish called the Devil's Hole pupfish can. It lives in a small pool at the bottom of a cave, in a North American desert. They struggle with floods, earthquakes and changing water levels, but people are helping them to survive.

Devil's Hole pupfish

## Should wild fish be kept as pets?

If fish are taken from the wild to be kept as pets, they may become rare in their natural home. If you set up a fish tank, it is best to choose common fish, which have never lived in the wild.

# Are giant tortoises rare?

**Yes – all giant tortoises live on just a few islands.** They are rare because tourists have disturbed them and passed on diseases. People have also brought cats and rats to the islands, which eat the giant tortoises' eggs.

Galapagos giant tortoise

# which frog can't croak?

The world's rarest frog, Hamilton's frog, can't croak. Unlike other frogs, it doesn't have webbed feet and it hatches from its egg as a tiny frog, instead of as a tadpole.

Hamilton's frog

## Turtle tears!

The noise and bright lights of beach hotels and bars can disturb rare green turtles and stop them laying eggs.

## Pretend

Put a basket on your back and see what it's like to carry your home like a giant tortoise!

# Why do salamanders need clean water?

Chinese and Japanese giant salamanders take in water through their skin and mouths. If the streams where they live are polluted, the salamanders take in the dirty water. This can make them ill and many may die.

17

# why are vultures in trouble?

Long-billed vulture

**Vultures are nature's very own clean-up crew.** They feed on the dead bodies of farm animals, which stops them rotting away and spreading diseases. Millions of vultures have died because a drug used to treat the farm animals is poisonous to the birds.

## Feed
Ask an adult to help you put out bird food, such as seeds and nuts.

# Why are parrots in danger?

Parrots are the most endangered birds. They are trapped illegally and sold as pets, and the forests where they live are being cut down. About one-third of all kinds of parrot are in danger.

## vanishing birds!

About one in every eight types of bird are in danger of becoming extinct. This means that about 1200 kinds of birds are likely to disappear in the coming years.

Scarlet macaw

# which bird is a good gardener?

In the rainforests of Australia, southern cassowaries spread the seeds of plants. The birds eat the plants, and the seeds come out in their droppings around the forest.

# Why are pandas in peril?

**Less than 2000 giant pandas live in the bamboo forests of China.** The forests are being cut down by people to build farms and roads. Pandas only eat bamboo, so they can't move to other forests.

Giant pandas

## Ferret families!

In 1987, wild black-footed ferrets were nearly extinct. Over 7000 babies have been born since, bringing them back from the danger of extinction.

Pygmy hog

## What is a pygmy hog?

The pygmy hog is the smallest, rarest pig. It was thought to be extinct, but a small number were saved and hundreds now live in a wildlife reserve. Baby hogs born in zoos are being released into the reserve.

### Visit

Take a trip to a zoo or wildlife park with your family. Do any endangered animals live there?

## Which hairy Australian needs protection?

The northern hairy-nosed wombat is very rare because its grassland home has been taken over by cattle. The last few live behind a tall fence, which protects them from dingos (wild dogs), which hunt them.

# why are jaguars special?

**Because they are beautiful and rare!** Jaguars are the biggest cats in the Americas. Even though they are protected, they are still hunted by people and their forest homes are being cut down.

Jaguar

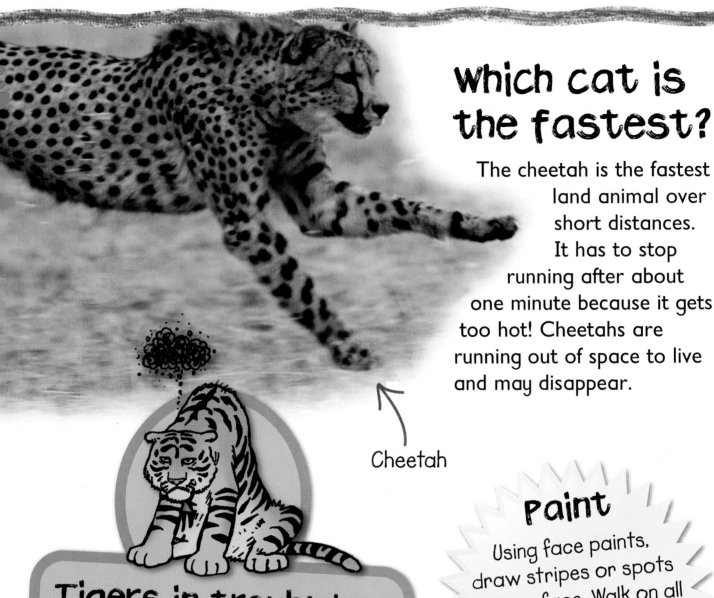

# which cat is the fastest?

The cheetah is the fastest land animal over short distances. It has to stop running after about one minute because it gets too hot! Cheetahs are running out of space to live and may disappear.

Cheetah

## Tigers in trouble!

About 100 years ago, there were probably more than 100,000 tigers in the world. Now there are only 3200 and their numbers are falling rapidly.

## Paint

Using face paints, draw stripes or spots on your face. Walk on all fours and pretend to be a tiger or a cheetah!

# what is the rarest cat?

The world's rarest cat is the Spanish, or Iberian, lynx. Its home has been destroyed and the rabbits it eats have been killed by diseases. There may be only about 100 of these beautiful cats left in the wild.

# which ape is the most endangered?

**Orang-utans are the most endangered apes.** Much of their forest home has been cut down. Huge areas of palm oil plants have replaced the trees, but the orang-utans can't live there.

Orang-utans

## save the animals!

If the forests where orang-utans live are protected, it will help thousands of other animals to survive as well. All forest animals depend on each other for survival.

# How can we help our chimp cousins?

Chimpanzees are probably the animal most closely related to us. To help them survive, wild nature reserves have been set up to protect them from hunters.

Chimp

## Make

Look at the chimp picture on this page and make a cardboard chimp face mask. Your mask will need big ears!

## Who guards gorillas?

Rare mountain gorillas are guarded by wardens in a national park in Africa, but this is dangerous work. The wardens may be injured or killed trying to save the last few wild mountain gorillas from hunters.

# Why are rhinos rare?

**Rhinos are rare because hunters kill them illegally and sell their horns.** The horns are used to make traditional medicines or handles for daggers. Wars and the loss of their natural homes also cause trouble for rhinos.

Rhinos

# what is a kouprey?

A kouprey, or grey ox, is a type of wild cattle that lives in the forests of Southeast Asia. Its numbers have fallen as low as perhaps 100, mainly because of hunting.

Kouprey

## Think

Elephants are not the only animals with tusks. Can you think of a sea animal that has tusks?

## Blackbuck pie!

Blackbuck antelope are doing so well on ranches in the USA that numbers have to be reduced! They are eaten in restaurants, and some are sent to India to increase numbers in the wild.

# Why are elephants in danger?

Elephants used be hunted for their valuable ivory tusks, and numbers are now half of what they were 30 years ago. Now the main problem is finding enough space for these huge animals to live alongside people.

# Are mountain gorillas safe?

Even though there are now over 700 mountain gorillas left in the wild, these gentle apes are still on the brink of extinction. They only live in one small area of Africa and are in danger from hunters and wars near their home.

Mountain gorilla

# can tourists help endangered animals?

Tourists can pay to watch and photograph animals in the wild. This money can be used to help save animals, such as cheetahs, from extinction. Organized safaris are one great way to get close to rare animals.

Cheetah

## rare penguin!

The yellow-eyed penguin is the rarest penguin. People are protecting them from predators such as dogs and planting coastal forests for them to nest in.

## Remember

Now you have read this book, see if you can remember the names of six endangered animals.

## which pigeon has gone forever?

Flocks of passenger pigeons once lived in North America. However millions of birds were shot and trapped, and their grassland homes were turned into farmland. Now passenger pigeons are extinct.

# Quiz time

**Do you remember what you have read about endangered animals?** Here are some questions to test your memory. The pictures will help you. If you get stuck, read the pages again.

3. Why do polar bears need ice?

page 8

4. Where do lemurs live?

page 10

1. Do eagles need our help?

page 5

5. Do seals wear fur coats?

page 13

2. Can we save the dodo?

page 7

page 14

6. Which dragon is in danger?

**7. Which frog can't croak?**

page 17

**8. Why are parrots in danger?**

page 19

**9. Which hairy Australian needs protection?**

page 21

**10. Why are jaguars special?**

page 22

**11. How can we help our chimp cousins?**

page 25

**12. Why are rhinos rare?**

page 26

**13. Which pigeon has gone forever?**

page 29

## Answers

1. Yes, because they are having trouble surviving
2. No, they are gone forever
3. They hunt on the ice, so they need it to live
4. On an island called Madagascar
5. No, but northern fur seals' fur was once used to make coats
6. The leafy sea dragon
7. Hamilton's frog
8. Because they are trapped illegally and sold as pets, and the forests where they live are being cut down
9. The northern hairy-nosed wombat
10. Because they are beautiful and rare
11. By setting up wild nature reserves to protect them from hunters
12. Because hunters kill them illegally and sell their horns
13. The passenger pigeon

31

# Index